TRIPLE H

AT THE TOP OF HIS GAME

by Sandy Donovan

Consultant:
Mike Johnson, Writer
PWInsider.com

CAPSTONE PRESS
a capstone imprint

Library of Congress Cataloging-in-Publication Data
Donovan, Sandra, 1967–
 Triple H : at the top of his game / by Sandy Donovan.
  p. cm.—(Velocity. Pro wrestling stars)
 Includes bibliographical references and index.
 Summary: "Describes the life of Triple H, both in and out of the ring"—Provided by publisher.
  ISBN 978-1-4296-8677-8 (library binding)
  ISBN 978-1-62065-362-3 (ebook pdf)
 1. Triple H, 1969—Juvenile literature. 2. Wrestlers—United States—Biography—Juvenile literature. I. Title.
GV1196.T75D66 2013
796.812092—dc23 [B]   2012011301

Editorial Credits
Mandy Robbins, editor; Sarah Bennett, designer; Laura Manthe, production specialist

Photo Credits
Alamy: Pictorial Press Ltd, 44; AP Images: Rick Scuteri, 31; Corbis: Chris Ryan, 38–39, Sygma/Uli Rose, 37, ZUMA Press/Matt Roberts, 42; Dreamstime: Deskcube, 15 (graphic hug); Getty Images: Moses Robinson, 41, Russell Turiak, 8, WireImage/Bob Levey, cover, WireImage/George Pimentel, 4–5, WireImage/KMazur, 30; Globe Photos: John Barrett, 13, 18, 24, 32; iStockphotos: grimgram, 17 (boxing ring), james steidl, 11, 14–15 (boxing ring); Newscom: ZUMA Press/Globe Photos, 20, 29, 35, ZUMA Press/UPN–TV/WWF, 36, 40; Photo by Wrealano@aol.com, 10, 22, 27; Shutterstock: Alice, 5 (crown), buriy, 43, Danomyte, 33, daveh900, 5 (stamp), debra hughes, 44 (cake), diez artwork, 19, Drozdowski, 12 (tea set), Eddies Images, 6–7 (dumbbells), elic, 14–15 (curtain), iQoncept, 16 (pass), James Steidl, 17 (crown), JungleOutThere, 45 (baby things), KRAFT STUDIO, 16 (stage), Maxx–Studio, 10 (phone), mutation, 9, Rozhkovs, 34 (timer), SimonasP, 40, 41 (crosses), VECTORACER, 34 (ladder), Volant, 5 (biceps/brain), WitR, 7 (weights); Wikimedia: Fatima, cover, 1 (background), GaryColemanFan, 12 (top)

Artistic Effects
Shutterstock

Printed in the United States of America in Stevens Point, Wisconsin.
032012   006678WZF12

TABLE of CONTENTS

THE GAME

Throughout his career Triple H has built a **legacy** as one of the greatest pro wrestlers of all time. And he has the record to back it up. Triple H has had an amazing run of championship titles since joining the World Wrestling Federation (WWF) in 1996. He has earned more than 20 championships. Triple H has also appeared in pro wrestling's biggest events since 1999.

In 2002 Triple H beat Chris Jericho to become the WWE Undisputed Champion.

legacy—the actions and reputation that a superstar is remembered for

Triple H earned his nickname "The Game" when he was at the top of his game. On the night of August 23, 1999, he defeated Mankind to win his first WWF Championship. Over the years, he's had plenty of other nicknames:

THE CONNECTICUT BLUE BLOOD

Rich, snobby people are often called "blue bloods." When Triple H first hit the WWF scene in the mid-1990s, he was known as Hunter Hearst Helmsley from Greenwich, Connecticut. He was called the Connecticut Blue Blood because people thought he was a snobby, rich jerk.

THE KING OF KINGS

This nickname comes directly from Motörhead's song "King of Kings." This song was one of Triple H's favorite entrance themes.

THE KING OF WWE

Triple H was never actually announced as "King of WWE." But he liked referring to himself that way. It was his way of telling people that he was better than anyone else in pro wrestling.

THE CEREBRAL ASSASSIN

"Cerebral" means brain and an assassin is a paid hit man. Triple H earned this nickname because of his reputation for being smarter than his opponents and for showing no mercy.

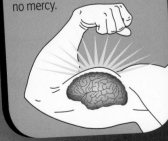

FACT

In 2002 WWF changed its name to World Wrestling Entertainment (WWE).

CHAPTER 1
THE EARLY YEARS

WEIGHING IN

How did young Paul Levesque transform himself into a heavyweight pro wrestling champion? It took a lot of hard work at the gym. But the payoff was huge. Paul's enormous size helped his career take off.

TRIPLE H TODAY

REAL NAME
Paul Levesque

HEIGHT
6 feet, 4 inches (193 centimeters)

WEIGHT
255 pounds (116 kilograms)

SIGNATURE MOVE
The Pedigree

JULY 27, 1969:
Paul Levesque was born in Nashua, New Hampshire.

EARLY 1980S: Paul was a skinny kid and a huge pro wrestling fan. His favorite superstar was Ric Flair.

1983: Paul went to a local gym and started working out every day. Soon he was hooked on bodybuilding and increased his weight to 135 pounds (61 kg). But it was just the beginning of Paul's weight gain.

1987: Paul graduated from high school and went on to enter bodybuilding contests. By then, he weighed in at more than 200 pounds (91 kg).

1989: Paul won Teenage Mr. New Hampshire. He worked as a manager at a local gym. But he dreamed of being a pro wrestler.

1991: Paul entered the famous professional wrestling training school of Walter Kowalski in Malden, Massachusetts.

1992: Under the stage name Terra Ryzing, Paul began his pro wrestling career. He wrestled in the Independent Wrestling Federation (IWF) league. In July Paul won the IWF Heavyweight Championship title.

FACT

As a pro wrestler, Paul's weight has been anywhere from 245 to 300 pounds (111 to 136 kg).

REACHING FOR HIS DREAM

Paul dreamed of wrestling for the powerful WWF. But he knew it would be hard to break into the top pro wrestling promotions company. In 1994 Paul tried out for a smaller company, World Championship Wrestling (WCW). Paul impressed the WCW officials. They offered him a two-year contract. But he still dreamed of making it to the WWF. Paul asked for a one-year contract instead. He hoped that a year of building up his skills at WCW would make him ready for the WWF.

Paul's first fight in WCW was on February 12, 1994. He entered the ring as Terra Ryzing, which was sometimes spelled Terror Rising or Terra Risin'. But soon Paul had a new ring name. He became Jean Paul Levesque, a snobby, rich French-Canadian. As Jean Paul, he sometimes teamed up with Lord Steven Regal, a snobby, rich British character.

As Jean Paul Levesque, Paul had a lot of practice looking down his nose at other wrestlers.

THE WWF, based in Stamford, Connecticut, began in 1963 as a spin-off of the National Wrestling Association (NWA). At the beginning, it was popular mostly in the northeastern states. But Chairman Vince McMahon worked to extend its reach across the United States. By the 1980s, the WWF was the most popular pro wrestling company in the world.

WCW got its start in Atlanta, Georgia, in 1989. At the beginning it was mostly popular in Georgia and other southeastern states. By the mid-1990s, WCW was the second most popular pro wrestling company. The most popular was the WWF. In 2001 the WWF bought out WCW.

Paul did well wrestling on **tag teams**, but he wanted to be known as a solo wrestler. The WCW officials didn't think he was good enough yet. Paul used his time there to practice his wrestling and his public speaking skills. He knew he'd need both to be a WWF superstar.

tag team—two or more wrestlers who partner together against other teams

PAUL'S BIG BREAK

Paul spent one year with WCW. During that year, he didn't think he received the publicity he deserved. Paul wanted to be a singles competitor. But WCW wouldn't let him.

Jean Paul Levesque

In late 1994, Paul's one-year contract with WCW was running out. Paul decided to make his move for the WWF. Paul convinced Vince McMahon to meet with him. He hoped to walk away with an offer to join the WWF. Paul thought the meeting went well. But he didn't get the job offer he had hoped for.

Paul decided to make the best of his time with WCW. In late December 1994, he fought at the WCW event *Starrcade* in Nashville, Tennessee. He lost to Alex Wright. But when he returned to his hotel that night, a huge surprise was waiting. Vince McMahon had called to offer him a job at WWF.

FACT

The December 1994 *Starrcade* fight against Alex Wright was Paul's pay-per-view TV **debut**. It was also his only pay-per-view event that year.

WWF

The offer Paul received from McMahon wasn't great. Paul was going to get paid less than he earned in WCW. But he had gotten his foot in the door at the WWF.

debut—someone's first public appearance

CHAPTER 2
THE BIRTH OF
HUNTER HEARST HELMSLEY

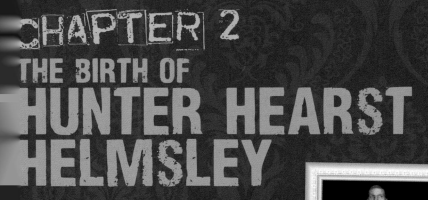

On April 29, 1995, Hunter Hearst Helmsley made his WWF debut. His snobby, rich character was similar to the French-Canadian Jean Paul Levesque, but Helmsley was all-American. He wore his long blond hair pulled back tightly in a ponytail, and he often appeared in all-black clothing.

Triple H's first nickname was "The Connecticut Blueblood." He also went by "The Greenwich Snob," a reference to a town in Connecticut. Even before his debut in the ring, he taped **vignettes**. In them Hunter discussed good manners and gave audiences a taste of his character.

vignette—a short video clip; vignettes are often used to introduce new characters to wrestling fans

THE KLIQ

Soon after joining the WWF, Triple H, Shawn Michaels, Diesel, Razor Ramon, and The 1-2-3 Kid formed a group called the Kliq. Though they were part of the same group, these men often wrestled as enemies. Triple H and Diesel were **heels**. Michaels, Ramon, and The 1-2-3 Kid were **babyfaces**. The Kliq was known for having a huge influence on WWF president Vince McMahon. Kliq members often got assigned to televised fights at popular events. In the mid-1990s, they were considered rising stars in the WWF.

Shawn Michaels (left) and Triple H (right) have fought many brutal matches over the years.

heel—a wrestler who acts as a villain in the ring

babyface—a wrestler who acts as a hero in the ring

CURTAIN CALL

In early 1996, things were going great for Triple H. He was beginning to make a splash in the WWF. But then his career took a bad turn. The Kliq got on Vince McMahon's bad side.

The event in question happened at New York City's Madison Square Garden. Razor Ramon and Diesel were leaving the WWF and going to WCW. They were set to fight their final matches on May 19, 1996. This event was called the Curtain Call. Triple H faced off against Ramon and won. Shawn Michaels defeated Diesel.

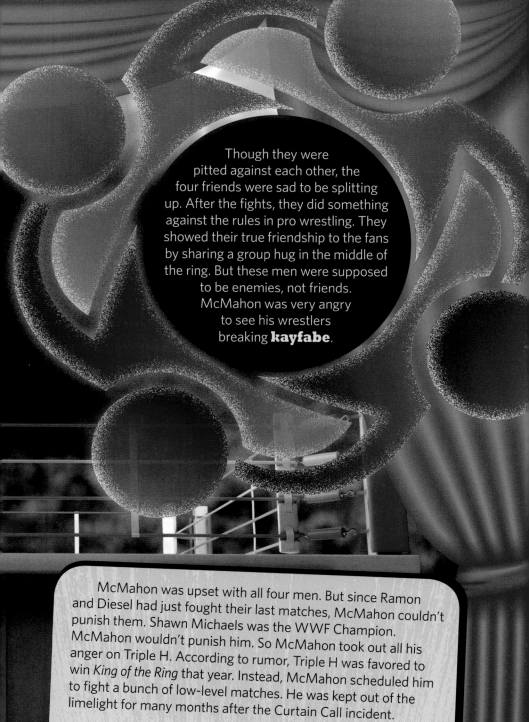

Though they were pitted against each other, the four friends were sad to be splitting up. After the fights, they did something against the rules in pro wrestling. They showed their true friendship to the fans by sharing a group hug in the middle of the ring. But these men were supposed to be enemies, not friends. McMahon was very angry to see his wrestlers breaking **kayfabe**.

McMahon was upset with all four men. But since Ramon and Diesel had just fought their last matches, McMahon couldn't punish them. Shawn Michaels was the WWF Champion. McMahon wouldn't punish him. So McMahon took out all his anger on Triple H. According to rumor, Triple H was favored to win *King of the Ring* that year. Instead, McMahon scheduled him to fight a bunch of low-level matches. He was kept out of the limelight for many months after the Curtain Call incident.

kayfabe—the practice of sticking to the story lines and keeping the real-life side of pro wrestling a secret

A WWF CHAMPION

Triple H knew he had to serve his punishment for breaking kayfabe. But he also knew his next chance would come around. And soon enough, it did. On October 21, 1996, Triple H fought Marc Mero for the Intercontinental Title on WWF's *Raw SuperShow*. Check out how it all went down:

BACKSTAGE

Triple H attacked Mr. Perfect. This was a direct challenge to fight. But Mr. Perfect wasn't cleared to wrestle that night. Marc Mero stepped in and volunteered to fight Triple H in Mr. Perfect's place.

MARC MERO

HEIGHT
6 ft, 1 in (185 cm)

WEIGHT
235 lbs (107 kg)

SIGNATURE MOVE
TKO (Total Knock Out)

IN THE RING

Triple H and Mero traded blows back and forth. At one point, Triple H slammed Mero into the mat. It looked like Mero was done for. Triple H grabbed a metal chair to finish Mero off. At this point, Mero's girlfriend, Sable, rushed in and grabbed the chair. Suddenly, Mr. Perfect showed up. He grabbed the chair and acted like he was going to hit Triple H with it. But then he turned and slammed Mero with it!

FOR THE WIN

Mero was exhausted. Triple H used his **signature move**, The Pedigree, on Mero. Then he pinned him for the win. Triple H was the new Intercontinental Champion!

3

signature move—the move a wrestler is best known for; sometimes called a finishing move

17

CHAPTER 3
TEAMING UP

It's hard to dominate in the world of pro wrestling without a little help from your friends. Triple H has had plenty of friends, starting with his first **bodyguard**, Chyna.

Chyna's amazing physical strength earned her the nickname "The Ninth Wonder of the World."

CHYNA

REAL NAME
Joanie Laurer

HEIGHT
5 ft, 10 in (178 cm)

WEIGHT
200 pounds (91 kg)

NICKNAME
The Ninth Wonder of the World

Chyna joined the WWF as Triple H's bodyguard in 1996. She helped him win by sneaking into the ring and going after his opponents. She often got away with using illegal moves when the referee wasn't looking.

Chyna was a huge factor in Triple H's early wins. One notable event happened during 1997's *King of the Ring* tournament. Triple H's first match was against Ahmed Johnson for the Intercontinental Championship. In that fight, Johnson was on the verge of winning when Chyna climbed up the outside of the ring and distracted him. That was all Triple H needed to take Johnson down for the win.

Chyna also helped Triple H overtake Mankind later on in the night. Triple H had done well throughout the match. But as Mankind was ready to make a comeback, Chyna smashed the King of the Ring **scepter** into his back. Shortly afterward, Triple H pinned Mankind for the win.

bodyguard—a person who goes to matches with another wrestler and helps him by surprising or ganging up on opponents; also called an enforcer

scepter—a rod or staff carried by a king or queen as a symbol of authority

BEST "FRENEMIES"

Triple H and Shawn Michaels became friends early on in their pro wrestling careers. It was Michaels who first used the name "Triple H" to describe his friend. He coined the name on the October 6, 1997, episode of *Raw*. Over the next 12 years, the pair sometimes teamed up with each other and sometimes **feuded** against each other. Check out their history full of highs and lows:

The duo were one of wrestling's most famous pairs when they formed the D-Generation X (DX) **stable**.

FRIENDS

1997

1998

After less than a year of DX, Triple H turned on Michaels. Triple H claimed that Michaels didn't pull his weight at *WrestleMania* in March 1998. Later that year, Michaels took some time off to heal after a back injury.

RIVALS

In 2006 the pair reunited for the new D-Generation X.

In 2009 they won their first-ever Tag Team Championship together.

2009

2006

2004

2002

In 2004 the duo had another fight. They faced off in a brutal **I LAST MAN STANDING MATCH**. In it, Michaels challenged Triple H for his World Heavyweight Championship belt. The match ended with both men being knocked out. Triple H got to keep his belt.

Michaels returned to WWE in 2002. At the beginning of a Raw broadcast, Triple H and Michaels came out in their DX uniforms. Just as they were about to perform their trademark entrance, Triple H attacked Michaels. A week later, Triple H smashed his former friend's face into a car window. At SummerSlam 2002, the pair met in an **I UNSANCTIONED STREET FIGHT**. Michaels won, but Triple H attacked him with a sledgehammer and nearly knocked him out.

LAST MAN STANDING MATCH

In this hardcore match there's only one way to win—by knockout. That means the winner has to strike hard enough to keep his opponent down for a count of 10. If this doesn't happen, the result is a "no-contest," which means no one wins.

UNSANCTIONED STREET FIGHT

These brutal match-ups take place outside the wrestling ring. They have no rules and often take place after the regularly scheduled fights have ended.

feud—to have a long-running quarrel between two people or groups of people

stable—a group of wrestlers who protect each other during matches and sometimes wrestle together; also called a faction

21

CHAPTER 4

FAMOUS FACTIONS

D-GENERATION X

DX was one of pro wrestling's most famous **factions**. The stable was known as a collection of heels, but they became fan favorites.

The 1998 version of DX included (from left to right) Billy Gunn, Road Dogg, Chyna, X-Pac, and Triple H.

1997-98: THE DEGENERATES RISE

The group consisted of Triple H, Chyna, Shawn Michaels, and Rick Rude. The stable got its start when the members started helping each other in the ring throughout 1997. One of their chief enemies, Bret Hart, famously said they were a bunch of degenerates, or low-lifes. The group combined the term "degenerate" with "generation X." Generation X is a title often used for people born in the 1960s and 1970s.

1998-99: DX TAKES A TURN

In 1998 Shawn Michaels left DX. Triple H formed a new version of DX with Chyna, X-Pac, Billy Gunn, and Road Dogg. The wrestlers were still heels, but the fans loved them. Some people considered them babyfaces. But by late 1999, with the addition of Tori, the stable was back to all heel, all the time. This was perfect for Triple H. He was much more comfortable as a heel than a babyface. By the end of 2000, however, DX had broken apart, and Triple H was a solo star.

2006 & 2009: DX REUNIONS

In June 2006, Triple H and Shawn Michaels reunited with as much heel energy as ever. This time, they turned their focus to making fun of Vince McMahon. Eventually, Michaels took some time away from wrestling. But in 2009, Triple H convinced him to return. They reunited as DX. They won their first match against a stable called Legacy at *SummerSlam* that year.

faction—a group of wrestlers who protect each other during matches and sometimes wrestle together; also called a stable

McMAHON-HELMSLEY FACTION

Triple H and Stephanie McMahon started out as a couple in the ring. This quickly turned into a relationship outside the ring as well.

Triple H and Vince McMahon were linked from the beginning of Triple H's WWE career. It was Vince who first hired Paul to wrestle in the WWF in 1995. The next year, they were in conflict after the Curtain Call incident. Eventually, the two were back on each other's good sides. But that was just the beginning of their up-and-down relationship. See how it went:

FACT

In 2002 Triple H and Stephanie's relationship was over in the wrestling ring. But they got married in real life in October 2003.

2011 Triple H took control of WWE. The WWE board elected him the Chief Operating Officer. In this position, Triple H "fired" his father-in-law, Vince.

2009 Triple H and the McMahons reunited against Randy Orton and his Legacy faction.

2002 Triple H's in-ring marriage to Stephanie was coming apart. By the end of 2002, the McMahon-Helmsley Faction was over.

2001 Triple H injured his leg and had to take nearly a year off from wrestling.

2000 By 2000 the McMahon-Helmsley Faction included many top WWF superstars. The Rock, Steve Austin, Undertaker, Kane, The Dudley Boyz, and Chris Jericho were all part of the group. Together, their goal was to help Triple H defend his championship title.

1999 The famous McMahon-Helmsley Faction began in 1999 as an **alliance** between Triple H and Stephanie McMahon. The two were feuding with Stephanie's father, Vince McMahon. To get at Vince, Triple H "married" Stephanie. Then he wrestled Vince and beat him at *Armageddon* that year. Soon Triple H and Vince ended their feud. Vince joined the McMahon-Helmsley Faction as a way of keeping WWF power within the family. For much of 1999, Triple H held the WWF Championship. At the same time, Stephanie McMahon held the Women's Championship.

alliance—an agreement between groups to work together

EVOLUTION

In early 2003 Triple H teamed up with his childhood idol, Ric Flair. Together with Batista and Randy Orton, they formed a new stable, Evolution. Evolution reminded some fans of Triple H's early days as the snobby Hunter Hearst Helmsley. All four Evolution members were known for their snobby personalities, custom-made suits, Rolex watches, and private jets.

In April 2003, Triple H and Ric Flair challenged Rob Van Dam and Kane for the World Tag Team title. Triple H and Flair came up short, but that didn't stop Evolution.

RIC FLAIR

REAL NAME
Richard Morgan Fliehr

HEIGHT
6 ft, 1 in (185 cm)

WEIGHT
243 pounds (110 kg)

SIGNATURE MOVES
Figure Four Leglock, Chop to the Chest

BATISTA

REAL NAME
David Michael Bautista Jr.

HEIGHT
6 ft, 6 in (198 cm)

WEIGHT
290 pounds (132 kg)

SIGNATURE MOVE
Batista Bomb

FACT

In all, the four members of Evolution have 42 World Championship titles between them. They have held 85 titles all together, have four *Royal Rumble* wins, and have appeared in more than 200 pay-per-view main events.

Evolution's shining moment came at *Armageddon* in December 2003. The main event that night was a **TRIPLE THREAT MATCH** for the World Heavyweight Championship. Triple H overcame Kane and Goldberg to walk away as World Heavyweight Champion. Meanwhile, Randy Orton beat Rob Van Dam for the Intercontinental Championship. Batista and Ric Flair also won the Tag Team Championship that same night. It was a triple slam for Evolution.

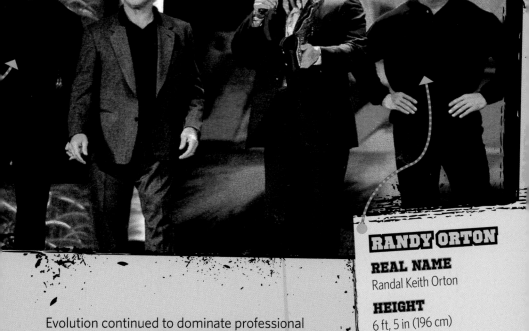

Evolution was made up of men of different ages because they were supposed to represent the best wrestlers from the past, present, and future of WWE.

Evolution continued to dominate professional wrestling through 2005. Some experts have called them the most powerful stable of all time.

RANDY ORTON

REAL NAME
Randal Keith Orton

HEIGHT
6 ft, 5 in (196 cm)

WEIGHT
235 pounds (107 kg)

SIGNATURE MOVES
RKO, Hanging DDT

27

CHAPTER 5

CHAMPION MATERIAL

In his long pro wrestling career, Triple H has won many championship titles. Check out some of his biggest victories:

INTERCONTINENTAL CHAMPIONSHIP

10/21/96
vs. Marc Mero

8/30/98
vs. The Rock

4/5/01
vs. Chris Jericho

4/16/01
vs. Jeff Hardy

WWF CHAMPIONSHIP

8/23/99
vs. Mankind

9/26/99
vacant title

1/3/00
vs. Big Show

5/21/00
vs. The Rock

3/17/02
vs. Chris Jericho

WORLD HEAVYWEIGHT CHAMPIONSHIP

9/2/02
named first champion

12/15/02
vs. Shawn Michaels

12/14/03
vs. Goldberg

9/12/04
vs. Randy Orton

1/9/05
vacant title

WWE CHAMPIONSHIP

10/7/07
vs. Randy Orton

4/27/08
vs. JBL, John Cena, and Randy Orton

2/15/09
Elimination Chamber

vacant—open; when a title is vacant, no one is currently holding it

KILLER MOVES

To be a champion in the world of pro wrestling, you need great signature moves. The Pedigree is Triple H's signature move. It has been described as a horizontal double-underhook piledriver. What's that? It's the single weapon that has helped Triple H earn a slew of championship titles. Here's how he does it:

THE PEDIGREE

1. Triple H gets his opponent hunched over at about a 70-degree angle.

2. Triple H puts his opponent's head between his legs and places his hand on the opponent's back.

3. Triple H pulls the opponent's arms behind his or her back.

MORE FAVORITE MOVES

In addition to The Pedigree, Triple H has many go-to moves in the ring. Here's how he performs a few of his most-used moves:

CHOP BLOCK

Triple H approaches his opponent from behind. He drives his shoulders into the back of the opponent's knees.

SPINEBUSTER

Triple H grabs his opponent around the waist. He lifts him and spins him 180 degrees. Then Triple H tosses the opponent onto his back—and often lands on top of him.

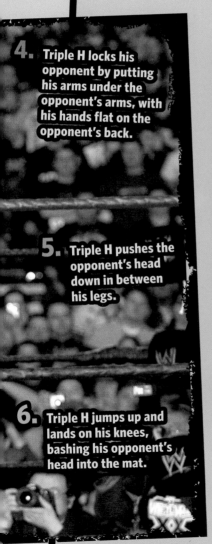

4. Triple H locks his opponent by putting his arms under the opponent's arms, with his hands flat on the opponent's back.

5. Triple H pushes the opponent's head down in between his legs.

6. Triple H jumps up and lands on his knees, bashing his opponent's head into the mat.

KNEE DROP

Triple H jumps up and lands on his opponent, painfully driving his knee into the opponent's body.

RUNNING HIGH KNEE

Triple H grabs his opponent's head. He pulls it down while bringing his own knee up to smash into the opponent's face.

RUNNING CLOTHESLINE

Triple H runs full-speed toward his opponent while holding his arm out straight and using it to knock down the opponent.

THE HARDER THEY FALL

Domination in the ring doesn't come without injuries. And the bigger a pro wrestler is, the harder he falls. But Triple H doesn't let injuries hold him back.

Triple H's attempt to help his friend resulted in a serious injury to himself.

Triple H's first major injury was during the May 21, 2001, episode of *Raw*. Triple H and Stone Cold Steve Austin were defending their Tag Team Championship against Chris Jericho and Chris Benoit. Jericho had Austin trapped in his signature move, the Walls of Jericho. Triple H rushed in to free his friend. In doing so, he tore his left **quadriceps** muscle nearly completely off his leg bone. Somehow Triple H still managed to finish the match, but he and Austin lost.

For most of 2010, Triple H suffered from pain in his neck and left shoulder. Doctors finally realized he had a torn **biceps** muscle. Triple H didn't know exactly when it happened, but he guessed it was probably while he was working out at the gym. Triple H underwent surgery to repair the torn muscle. After several months off, he was back in the ring again.

quadriceps—a muscle in the front part of the thigh

biceps—the large muscle at the front of the arm between the shoulder and inner elbow

FACT

After Triple H tore his quadriceps muscle, he needed an operation. He took more than eight months off from wrestling to allow his injury to heal.

CHAPTER 6

FEARSOME FEUDS

Triple H has wrestled for nearly 20 years. In that time, he's had his share of ongoing fights with rival wrestlers.

TRIPLE H VS. THE ROCK

In 1998 these two rising superstars faced off at *SummerSlam*. They competed in a **LADDER MATCH** for the Intercontinental Championship. After a back-and-forth duel, Triple H came out the winner.

Soon The Rock teamed up with Mankind to form a tag team called The Rock 'n' Sock Connection. They directly challenged Triple H and D-Generation X. And at *WrestleMania* 2000, Triple H successfully defended his WWE Championship title from The Rock. But The Rock came back at *Backlash* later that year. With a little help from Stone Cold Steve Austin, the Rock took the WWE Championship from Triple H. At *Judgment Day* 2000, Triple H faced off against The Rock again in an **IRON MAN MATCH**. Triple H came out victorious to claim the championship belt again.

IRON MAN MATCH

In an Iron Man Match, two fighters wrestle for a set number of minutes—usually 30 or 60. During that time, the referee calls decisions for pins and other victories. Whoever has the most decisions at the end of the time is the winner.

LADDER MATCH

In a Ladder Match, two wrestlers fight it out to reach a championship belt hanging high above the ring. Their only prop is a ladder placed under the belt. Whoever scales the ladder first and grabs the belt claims victory.

THE ROCK

REAL NAME
Dwayne Johnson

HEIGHT
6 ft, 5 in (196 cm)

WEIGHT
260 pounds (118 kg)

SIGNATURE MOVES
Rock Bottom, People's Elbow

Triple H and The Rock faced off many times over the years.

TRIPLE H VS. STONE COLD STEVE AUSTIN

Triple H and Stone Cold Steve Austin first faced each other in October 1996. Austin defeated Triple H.

Things heated up at *SummerSlam* in 1999 when Triple H hit Austin with a steel chair. Mankind ended up defeating both Triple H and Austin in the three-way match. But the feud was on. Triple H and Austin had a rematch at *No Mercy* that same year. Triple H won after The Rock pounded Austin with a sledgehammer. The really annoying part for Austin was that The Rock had been trying to hit Triple H!

For *Survivor Series* 1999, Triple H, Austin, and The Rock were scheduled to fight again. But Triple H paid another wrestler, Rikishi, to injure Austin. The attack knocked Austin out of the competition for the night.

Triple H and Austin faced each other again at *Survivor Series* in 2000. This time Triple H tried to get Austin to follow him out to the parking lot. Triple H got into his car and was ready to hit Austin with it. But Triple H didn't know that Stone Cold had jumped into a forklift. Using the forklift, Austin lifted up Triple H's car and flipped it on its roof—with Triple H inside!

The next year, the feud ended in a Three Stages of Hell match. These matches feature a best-of-three winner. Two wrestlers fight three times. The first to win twice is the match champion. Triple H beat Austin two falls to one.

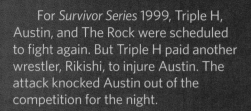

STONE COLD STEVE AUSTIN

REAL NAME
Steve Williams

HEIGHT
6 ft, 2 in (188 cm)

WEIGHT
252 pounds (114 kg)

SIGNATURE MOVE
Stone Cold Stunner

"THE TWO MAN POWER TRIP"

In 2001 former rivals Triple H and Stone Cold came together. They formed a tag team called The Two Man Power Trip. At the time, Triple H was the Intercontinental Champion. Austin was the WWF Champion. Together they defeated Kane and Undertaker to win the World Tag Team Championship. It was only the second time in history that one tag team held all three top WWF titles.

37

TRIPLE H VS. SHEAMUS

In 2006 a new WWE wrestler named Sheamus made his pay-per-view debut on *Monday Night Raw*. He was part of a team charged with booting D-Generation X from their ringside seats. Instead, Triple H took him out with a Pedigree. For several years after that, the two didn't cross paths. But in 2010, a feud erupted.

SHEAMUS

REAL NAME
Stephen Farrelly

HEIGHT
6 ft, 4 in (193 cm)

WEIGHT
267 lbs (121 kg)

SIGNATURE MOVE
Brogue Kick, High Cross

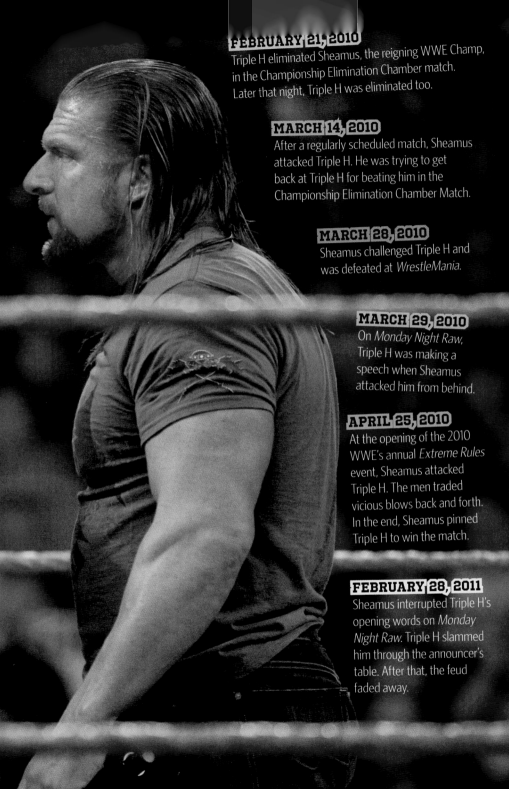

FEBRUARY 21, 2010
Triple H eliminated Sheamus, the reigning WWE Champ, in the Championship Elimination Chamber match. Later that night, Triple H was eliminated too.

MARCH 14, 2010
After a regularly scheduled match, Sheamus attacked Triple H. He was trying to get back at Triple H for beating him in the Championship Elimination Chamber Match.

MARCH 28, 2010
Sheamus challenged Triple H and was defeated at *WrestleMania*.

MARCH 29, 2010
On *Monday Night Raw*, Triple H was making a speech when Sheamus attacked him from behind.

APRIL 25, 2010
At the opening of the 2010 WWE's annual *Extreme Rules* event, Sheamus attacked Triple H. The men traded vicious blows back and forth. In the end, Sheamus pinned Triple H to win the match.

FEBRUARY 28, 2011
Sheamus interrupted Triple H's opening words on *Monday Night Raw*. Triple H slammed him through the announcer's table. After that, the feud faded away.

CHAPTER 7

TRIPLE H STYLE

Throughout his career, Triple H has changed his style more often than his nicknames. In his early days as The Connecticut Blue Blood, he wore his long hair combed back smoothly in a ponytail and sported long black pants.

Once he joined DX, he became a ripped T-shirt and leather-wearing tough guy. His hair, cut a little shorter, was messy and in his face.

In the early 2000s, Triple H dyed his hair even blonder as a mega heel. He wore it straight back in a neat ponytail again.

From 2003 to 2005, Triple H was back to fancy suits and swanky jewelry. His style matched that of the other three Evolution members.

Today nothing stands out on Triple H more than the Iron Cross symbol. Triple H displays this symbol of power most times he enters the ring. The Iron Cross is a famous German military symbol. It was used from the early 1800s through 1945. Today this symbol is popular with motorcyclists, punk rockers, and bands like Metallica and Motörhead—two of Triple H's favorite bands.

Triple H sports the Iron Cross in the front and back of his trunks and on the outsides of his boots.

ENTRANCE THEMES

As Triple H's image has changed, so have his entrance themes. Check out the explosive musical selections that have ushered Triple H into the arena.

From 1995 to 1996, Triple H entered the ring to **"BLUE BLOOD."** This song was written by longtime WWF composer Jim Johnston. The title left no doubt as to which wrestler it's about.

From 1996 to 1997 Triple H entered to **"ODE TO JOY"** by Ludwig van Beethoven. This classic piece of music was perfect for rich, snobby Hunter Hearst Helmsley.

In 1999 one of Triple H's entrance themes was **"CORPORATE PLAYER"** by Jim Johnston. Johnston wrote it to highlight Triple H's new closeness to the McMahon corporation. Triple H's arrival in the ring to this song marked the beginning of the McMahon-Helmsley Faction.

Another of Triple H's entrance themes in 1999 was **"HIGHER BRAIN PATTERN"** by Jim Johnston. Triple H entered to this song when he was highlighting his smart bad-guy style. He also wanted to complement his new nickname, The Cerebral Assassin.

From 1999 to 2000 Triple H entered to **"MY TIME"** by Chris Warren. Warren is the lead singer and songwriter for the DX Band. He wrote this song to back up Triple H's claim that it was his time to dominate the WWF.

Since 2001 Triple H has frequently entered the ring to the song **"THE GAME"** by Motörhead. The Texas band Drowning Pool performs another version of this song, which Triple H also uses.

Another Motörhead song that Triple H enjoys is **"KING OF KINGS."** He never actually entered the ring to this song. But it has been used in his short promo videos since 2006.

In 2011 Triple H began using the song **"FOR WHOM THE BELL TOLLS"** by Metallica. It was the backdrop for his entrance at *WrestleMania*.

43

CHAPTER 8

REAL LIFE VS. REEL LIFE

In 2003 Paul Levesque and Stephanie McMahon were married.

Triple H's fame in the WWE ring has led to many opportunities outside of the ring. He has appeared in movies and has also made appearances on TV. Triple H also focuses on his family and on the future of WWE.

FAMILY LIFE

1999   2001

REEL LIFE

In 1999 Triple H played a pro wrestler on *The Drew Carey Show.*

Triple H played an ex-criminal turned family man in *The Chaperone.*

In 2001 Triple H appeared on the sketch comedy show *MADtv.*

In 2008 Stephanie gave birth to their second daughter, Murphy Claire, on July 28.

In 2010 Paul and Stephanie's third daughter, Vaughn Evelyn, was born on August 24.

Later that year Paul took over as senior advisor of new talent development for WWE. He helps the company find and recruit new wrestlers.

In 2006 Paul and Stephanie's first daughter, Aurora Rose Levesque, was born on July 24.

003 | 2004 | 2005 | 2006 | | 2008 | | 2010 | 2011

In 2004 Triple H played a thug named Jarko Grimwood in the movie *Blade: Trinity*.

In 2005 Triple H appeared as himself on *The Bernie Mac Show*.

In 2011 Triple H appeared in two movies: *The Chaperone* and *Inside Out*.

Paul Levesque went from a scrawny kid to the King of Kings inside the ring. What's next for The Game? Only time will tell.

GLOSSARY

alliance (uh-LY-uhnts)—an agreement between groups to work together

babyface (BAY-bee-fayss)—a wrestler who acts as a hero in the ring

biceps (BYE-seps)—the large muscle on the front of the arm between the shoulder and inner elbow

bodyguard (BOD-ee-gard)—a person who goes along to matches with another wrestler and helps that wrestler out by surprising or ganging up on opponents; also called an enforcer

debut (DAY-byoo)—a person's first public appearance

faction (FAK-shun)—a group of wrestlers who take the same side in a dispute; also called a stable

feud (FYOOD)—a long-running quarrel between two people or groups of people

heel (HEEL)—a wrestler who acts as a villain in the ring

kayfabe (KAY-faybe)—the practice of sticking to the story lines and keeping the real-life side of wrestling a secret

legacy (LEG-uh-see)—qualities and actions one is remembered for

quadriceps (KWAH-druh-seps)—a muscle in the front part of the thigh

scepter (SEP-tur)—a rod or staff carried by a king or queen as a symbol of authority

signature move (SIG-nuh-chur MOOV)—the move a wrestler is best known for; sometimes called a finishing move

stable (STAY-buhl)—a group of wrestlers who protect each other during matches and sometimes wrestle together

tag team (TAG TEEM)—two wrestlers who partner together against other teams

vacant (VAY-kuhnt)—open; a vacant title is not held by anyone

vignette (vin-YET)—short video clips, vignettes are often used to introduce new characters to wrestling fans

READ MORE

Kaelberer, Angie Peterson. *The Fabulous, Freaky, Unusual History of Pro Wrestling.* Unusual Histories. Mankato, Minn.: Capstone Press, 2011.

Shields, Brian. *Triple H.* DK Readers. New York: DK Publishing, 2009.

Skog, Jason. *Kurt Angle: From Olympian to Wrestling Machine.* Pro Wrestling Stars. North Mankato, Minn.: Capstone Press, 2013.

INTERNET SITES

FactHound offers a safe, fun way to find Internet sites related to this book. All of the sites on FactHound have been researched by our staff.

Here's all you do:

Visit *www.facthound.com*

Enter this code: 9781429686778

INDEX